15 YEARS ARE PLENTY

15 YEARS ARE PLENTY

By The MortgageMInuteGuy
ROGER SCHLESINGER

authorHOUSE®

AuthorHouse™ LLC
1663 Liberty Drive
Bloomington, IN 47403
www.authorhouse.com
Phone: 1-800-839-8640

Published by AuthorHouse   11/09/2013

ISBN: 978-1-4918-1399-7 (sc)
ISBN: 978-1-4918-1398-0 (hc)
ISBN: 978-1-4918-1397-3 (e)

Library of Congress Control Number: 2013916288

"Everyone has, I think, in some quiet corner of his mind, an ideal home waiting to become a reality."

—Paige Rense, Editor, Architectural digest

It's Not Your Uncle Bob's Mortgage— But It Ain't Bad.

Oh, Uncle Bob paid off his $200,000 house (current value) because he got his loan right after World War II. He swears by the 30 year fixed mortgage. He'll tell you all about it time and time again over Thanksgiving turkey. So let's go back and find out why Uncle Bob is so sure this is right for you, too.

The 30-year fixed began in the 1930's, decades before the 15 year fixed was introduced. It wasn't until the 70's that we saw variable interest rate loans, with hybrids, and fixed loans that adjusted. In the 80's, we saw adjustable (variables) that are fixed for a period.

But Uncle Bob had one choice. The 30-year fixed was an arranged marriage, and he had to take her. Thus, his expertise is rather limited. (No offense to your Aunt).

Now that I've ruled out Uncle Bob's advice, (besides, he always shows up to Thanksgiving with a questionable salad anyway,) let me save you money. In fact, let me save you a lot of money. If you read every page of this book, you should save thousands. I've broken it down to 50 simple points, highlighted to help you find the information you're looking for to help you make the right choice.

ECONOMICS (note, this is a highlighted point . . .)

Economists are those rare professionals who can never be wrong (or right for that matter). It's an art, not a science, and results are subject to whomever is giving them.

Economists have the luxury of taking their theory, contradictory to each other as they may be, and automatically finding a home. If you're one way, you go Republican; if you're the other way, you go Democrat. Oh, if only all professions could be so simple.

But an economist is the epitome of the slogan, "what have you done for me lately? An expert can be right (or at least not wrong) for years and make one bad calculation, and he's suddenly yesterday's news. An amateur can make a wild/lucky on the mark statement, and he's the new messiah over night; that's what you get in an industry without standards.

Author's note: I have a Bachelor of Arts Degree (B.A.) in Economics from U.C.L.A.

Bottom line: Economics can go either way. It can help you if you research enough, and it may hinder you should you choose to ignore the mountain of information. But the best of the best contradict one another; it's just not a place to hang your hat.

The World Is Not My Problem

You turn on Fox or CNBC only to find the following: Asia's market takes a dive. Russia's funneling billions to private banks. Europe is ganging up on itself. South America is trying to go sober. So what should you do?

Fret not. That's it. Fret not. Whatever interest rates you're staring at right now are all that matter. The rest of the world is out of your control (assuming you're not one of those creeps pilfering the Russian money.) If you are—hey, thanks for buying my book anyway.

There are plenty of reasons to enter the mortgage arena including buying a house, refinancing your current mortgage, consolidating several loans, or pulling cash out of you property. If Japan eats South Africa, it shouldn't change your situation any time soon.

If your main reason to act is to lower your interest rate, then you're in for a nervous stomach. Interest rates must be right (now) for you to make your move.

My World Is Me

Your potential economic future is the one dictating force behind acquiring a new mortgage. Your job prospect, your earning potential, your retirement goals are singularly important, and every other outside force is irrelevant unless it relates directly to you.

The neighbor's dog, your mother-in-law, and the fact that airline seats seem to be getting smaller as your cushion gets larger, are all distractions in life. Nonetheless, don't let them distract you from your goal.

Know where you're going so you don't end up where you're heading. Sales leaders have always chided their sales people to plan their work and then work their plan. Your life is much the same. If you have a destination in mind, detours on the way to getting through can be easily dealt with. It's those people who don't know where they are heading who can easily get lost, and they do. Don't let that be you.

Inflation-Deflation, So What?!

It comes and goes, like relatives who visit more often than you like. And you're never sure how long they'll stay. It's that scary word—inflation. Is high inflation something you need to deal with or someone else's problem? Can it affect your way of living, or does that only happen to the big boys?

Like those relatives who eat all your food and drink all your beer, you need to stand up to inflation. Some inflation/deflation can mess up a well-conceived plan or even poorly conceived ones by the economic realities that occur in the economy during those times. It all boils down to one phrase which is a truth of Biblical proportions in the home-buying world. Ignore it, and you'll end up in mortgage hell. That phrase is as follows: you cannot have high interest rates without rising home prices. You might see times of home prices rising without inflation but probably never the other way around.

Fear causes people to paint a picture of a world where interest rates skyrocket while home prices remain steady, and this leads them to conclude that long term fixed rates are the only safe solution. If you know, however, that home prices will follow inflation, and that increased home equity will cause many people to sell or refinance and pull money out, then it's easy to understand why there's no reason to pay extra for a long term fixed rate. It feels safe but isn't well thought out.

When you decide to delve into economics, try to uncover all the facts and set the right parameters to reach an intelligent conclusion that works for you.

<u>What if We Lose the Tax Deduction on Our Mortgage?</u>

This could be a real dilemma if the push to a real balanced budget continues. The only way to plan for this contingency is by developing a strategy to pay off your loan.

Many believe the interest rates will decrease when and if the deductibility of said rates are eliminated. Let me remind you of the unleaded gas story. Before unleaded gas was introduced to the market place, the oil companies told us it would be cheaper because they didn't have to add the lead. When

the cars converted to unleaded, we were then told
prices went up because they had to remove the
lead. The people in control are always looking for
a way to squeeze another buck out of you, and
they almost always will. Your job is to outsmart
them. And there's only one way to do this: pay off
your mortgage. They are then left helpless. The
politicians will be forced to go and sue the tobacco
companies one more time to make up the extra cash.

Throughout this book, I'll give you tips on how to
do this, but there are alternative viewpoints. While
none maybe as good as mine, I will present them
should you not want to pay off your mortgage.
One concept states that you can't borrow money
as cheaply as you can on your home so why pay it
off?" These folks are merely talking to the big boys
as most people will need the equity in their home
to supplement social security to be able to survive
the latter years. Be sure to create the equity before
you need it and don't count on appreciation as your
salvation.

CREDIT

What's Good/Bad Credit on a Home Loan?

The mortgage business is both similar to and also unlike any other business. In the "like other businesses" category, what occurs in the mortgage industry is paramount to you credit while incidences in other industries are less relevant. The industry differs from others because money cannot change certain factors such as a discount of the rate based on a particular credit score. In other words, you cannot buy the rate down without the score.

Allow me to define a few types of credit:

1. Good credit is 12 to 24 months of perfect mortgage payments. Bad credit is foreclosures, deeds-in-lieu and late payments. "My dog ate my payment" has even less a chance of working with a lender than it did with your second grade teacher.

2. Excellent credit is a credit report devoid of lates with small credit balances in relation to higher credit limits and a small number of revolving accounts. Lenders like to believe, true or not, that you can afford you payments.

3. Poor credit is a report with lates on revolving and installment accounts in the last 12-24 months and late payments on your current home loan. The individual's credit deteriorates as lates go from 30 days to 60 or 90 days. If you're getting calls from your creditor, you're likely in the 30-day category. If you cringe when those calls come in, you're probably in the 60-day category. If you've ripped your phone out of the wall, odds are you're in the 90-days plus category.

Irrelevancies are paid judgments and state or federal tax liens that are paid. In most cases, bankruptcies and foreclosures that are over three to four years old and short pays over two years can be disregarded. This is strictly a function of the lender.

Your credit can cost you money if you don't understand what is good and what is bad in the mortgage industry. An automobile repossession that is over 5 years old is minor, especially if there isn't a balance showing, but a house repossession without a loss to the lender can be huge! Lenders are allergic to repossessions, deeds-in-lieu of foreclosures, short pays or a straight foreclosure. It's like cat hair, a bee sting, dust, milk, and peanuts all rolled into one. If the allergy items are on your report, you need help. It's out there. Give it a search. In fact, right after you're done reading this book, make a note.

Credit Scores

Much like an in-law, everyone has a credit score, whether you want one or not. When your credit is processed along with the actual report, there comes one or more credit scores. These numbers, at a point, are really out of your control.

Most lenders look at your credit score in determining your credit worthiness. The number one credit scoring company, The Fair Isaacs Co. (FICO), developed a secret formula akin to Colonel Sanders secret recipe of herbs and spices, and it can help you in processing a home loan but without all the deadly grease. The lenders with the best rates require a minimum FICO score and in some cases will reduce the interest on these loans for high scores. It's similar to how high scoring basketball players get out of trouble where you and I can't.

Conforming loans can have a minimum, and it's generally 620. A Jumbo's minimum is generally 640. The current parameter of scores for the primary borrower (the one who makes the most money) are as follows:

620—Minimum for most good lenders. You'll get a loan, but they may act like they're doing you a favor on par with France giving us the Statue of Liberty.

720—Reduced interest rate, baby! (Generally only with a loan to value of 60% or less).

There are a number of ways to help your score, from closing inactive revolving accounts to bringing down your balances on open accounts. Should you live right and pay your bills on time, life and your credit score should be okay.

Pro Active Repair

The easiest way to take care of bad credit is to rid yourself of the obligation and, three to six months later, begin a letter writing campaign to the various credit gathering agencies denying ever having been late. The law states that the credit reporting agency must investigate each inquiry and remove the inquiry if the creditor doesn't confirm the information within a 30-day period. Since your obligation has been paid, the information is now most likely in storage and not readily accessible. It's a lot of work to take Sally away from her job of calling people and threatening to ruin their lives for being late in their payments and then having to send her down the hall to search for your records. The derogatory credit will have to be removed if not challenged within 30 days.

Trust me, it's worth the effort; I have client's who have saved millions by taking the time to clean up their credit and refinance after the fact.

Co-Signers

Co-signers are desired by FHA and can also be used on Freddie Mac programs. A strong non-occupying co-signer can make the package go from weak to strong. If lack of money for down payment is your problem, have the co-signer gift you money and keep them off the loan.

B.K. or Foreclosure

Bubonic Plague or Black Death? Take your pick. These are mere colds if you're getting a car loan, but a house loan turns them into killers. If you're the unfortunate recipient of either, consider yourself quarantined for a while.

The best lenders won't look at you for a minimum of four years, if at all, while these blotches are on your credit. As far as they're concerned, you're infectious, ugly, and chew with your mouth open.

Some of the intermediate lenders who are not as strict but whose rates are not as good will consider you after as little as a year but generally after two years; V.A. loan consideration is 2 years.

A late payment after one of these disasters sets you back even further. The best lenders will turn and run like a vegetarian at The Outback.

Just because you made an error, your fault or an act of God, doesn't force you into servitude for life. You can right the ship and sail on.

LTV Makes it Right

Loan to value is the key to any lender. The lower the loan to value, the easier it is to make the loan. If your father-in-law is kind enough to sell you his $750,000 home for a measly $400,000, odds are good you'll get the loan. The bank will be licking its chops should you not make your payments, and your father-in-law will subject you to a lifetime of I-told-you-so's.

The old equalizer is equity. The greater the equity there is in your home, the easier it is to get a loan even with outstanding problems. The more equity the less risk to the lender.

The magic number is generally a loan at 65% LTV or less. Most lenders will give you some credit that will lower the interest rate for loans with this much equity in the property. They might even shake your hand and call you "sir".

This leads me to why I like the 15 year fixed. You can achieve this type of equity with a 15-year loan in as little as 7 years without relying on appreciation. Should you hit the right interest rate market or a rapidly appreciating real estate market, you might be able to cut into the 7 years.

Like diamonds to women, nothing rules the mortgage industry like equity, and smart borrowers don't rely on inflation to create equity. Amortization is now king. To maximize amortization, you need to lower the interest rate and shorten the term of the loan. Once that's in place then, with luck, you might be able to add rising prices and watch the equity grow. It's a jewelry store!

PURCHASES

There are millions of homes purchased every year, from big mansions with gated entries to tiny, leaky houses under bridges, and the overwhelming majority need a mortgage to close the deal. Less than half of the houses are purchased for 100 percent cash.

The type of mortgage that is right for you is as personal as your DNA, so why are the majority of all loans 30 year fixed? That's basically a brunette boy with no real great skills and a bland personality.

The right home mortgage fits the family like a good son who calls his mother every weekend. The wrong one is like the kid who drops out of school, lives off you for 35 years, and never gives you grandkids.

The Loan is Equally as Important as the House

How many times have I heard a borrower tell me the following: "Get me a loan—any loan! I need to close this house!" You might as well cover yourself in blood and dive into a pool of sharks. The house that you so wanted will suddenly get ugly when you can't make the payments or, at best, you're locked into a loan that isn't accomplishing what you need.

What if your house depreciates and so does your equity? Or what if your five year plan to move up is going to take two to three times as long because you don't have sufficient equity? Suddenly, your aunt's offer to move in and bring her 3 kids for the price of a little rent doesn't look so bad. Now you know you're in trouble.

Get the loan right from the start, and the house will work. If you start house first and then try to let the loan take care of itself, you've parachuted into the middle of a landmine.

Save yourself the trouble—take notes on my next point.

Prequalification—A Free Look for Both sides

In today's complex and fast moving world, realtors always present a prequalification letter along with their offer to assure the seller that the buyer is qualified to purchase the home. The problem is that many realtors will simply call a buddy for a prequalification letter so he or she can present the offer. It's a troublesome part of the business that hurts the buyer more than anyone.

A prequal gives the lender and the borrower a free look. Don't worry about the lender—worry about yourself and use wisely that time before you make the offer and go into contract. This is the time to study the programs and see if your lender of choice has the type of program you need. If not, you have time to move on and find the right lender for you.

This time to think and make the right move is precious before the offer is accepted; it shouldn't be wasted. Once it's a go, the time is very dear. The best advice I have for you is to use your time wisely.

It can mean the difference between a good loan or a very costly one, a time of joy or a frustrating phone call to your lawyer who'll charge you $300 an hour just to say "didn't you read Roger's book?"

Start Right—End Right

There's an old saying in poker—"You can't win them all unless you win the first hand," and so it is with home financing. There's another saying in bullfighting that goes, "You can't win all of them unless you win the first one," but it's not quite that bad in home financing.

The start of the loan sets the tone of winning with our mortgage. A fixed rate fully amortized loan with a shorter duration (20 years or less) is ideal but not usually the one offered. If you didn't get that, don't feel bad, there are plenty of people in Mensa who never figured that one out.

If it's a low start rate you're looking for, consider taking a variable with a low payment for several years. If you then pay more than necessary, you can really dig into your loan balance. That's a great direction to go—heading toward paying off your loan. That, my friend, is where you reap. That, my friend, is the final goal: no payments and a house you enjoy. From there, all you need is a big screen TV, a reliable remote and a bag of chips. As for you women, I can't say I know exactly what is your need, but I'm getting better from raising two daughters and from now gaining grand-daughters at a steady pace.

Don't succumb to the temptation to pay a little at the beginning and grow into your loan later. This is an idea straight from the devil himself. You'll be years behind and you'll wonder what in Hades happened. It's better to buy a lesser property and do the loan right than stretch for a house out of reach and be forced into an inferior loan.

PMI or Piggyback?

Wanna see hives on a lender? Tell them you want to put less than 20 percent down. And they don't particularly like hives—it makes them charge you more in one of three ways: A higher rate, private mortgage insurance (PMI) or a second T.D. behind the first mortgage to reach the desired loan to value. A second T.D. is always trickier, Fixed or HELOC (Home Equity Line of Credit). If interest rates are lower, go fixed, if they are higher, go variable, and always assume that low rates will go higher and high rates will go lower and act accordingly.

When you opt for a higher rate or PMI, you almost always need to refinance when the desired level of 80 percent is reached. Minimum, you will need an appraisal to prove to the lender you've arrived at an LTV where PMI doesn't survive, and don't expect the mortgage insurer or lender to voluntarily reduce the rate or remove the mortgage insurance.

A second T.D. is best if you feel you will be able to pay the loan down eventually and remain with just the first mortgage. If you can't pay it off when you need too, go for a fixed 2nd for a long period of time.

In any case, make sure you evaluate the circumstances before you choose and consider both the short and long term ramifications.

Don't Close on Monday

You can't close a real estate transaction unless all finances are in place the day before it closes. The minute the lender puts the money in place, the interest clock begins. That's right, the meter is ticking before the actual close.

Should you close on Monday or the day after a holiday, you're paying additional interest for a day or two on your loan. That's cash you could have kept.

If this money isn't significant enough to matter to you, buy several copies of this book for friends whom you care about like me!

When Do I Lock?

That is a rare question indeed yet a very smart one. You can lock your loan when you fill out your application or any time between then and the approval of your loan. Once the loan is approved, you can get a better rate or lower cost or, perhaps, both.

Lock now. This is the time. Unless, like some drunken frat boy sitting outside the bathroom, you just can't wait for loan approval.

Similar to that analogy, the time to close is not always in your control. Shoot for the end of the month, when lenders are trying to up their closing numbers and might be willing to take it easier on you to help make their numbers!

Prepare Your Down Payment Early

The down payment is the money you are going to put into the transaction. You probably know that. But what you might not know is that lenders want at least a 90-day paper trail on that money. They want to believe you didn't hold up a bank to get the cash. Should you need to hold up a bank to get the cash, do it in a year advance, so the money's been sitting in your account all along.

Lenders don't like people who borrow money for a down payment. If the cash has been there awhile, they won't know how you got it. The IRS is a different story. I'll write that book another day.

So go get that money NOW. If you are getting a gift, get it early; otherwise, the gift giver will feel like he went through an MRI to prove they had the money. It will save time and alleviate problems. If finding the right property takes a while, the down payment will be sitting there waiting.

<u>Look for the Deals</u>

The deals are out there, baby. Don't miss them. There's always some lender who's desperately seeking a purchaser and will offer great incentives. Some will give cash grants. Others will promise to pay all the closing costs. Some of this is government dictated.

How do you find these deals? Read the financial publications and look at the advertisements.

Work with pros who can get the job done. A deal is worth pursuing because you can save thousands of dollars.

You might find it necessary to look in a different locale, community or county, but the savings can certainly be worth the effort.

Basically, you're looking for money, and it's there. And it's yours. And you'll find it. How's that for incentive?

Non Re-Occurring Closing Costs—How Not to Pay Them

Closing costs include the following: escrow or attorney closes, title insurance (generally on the loan only, at a reduced rate), lender fees on the loan, appraisal and credit. Add to that the points you may decide to pay (probably not a good idea,) and you have the entire package.

Never make an offer on a property without including a clause for a credit of $5,000 to $10,000 for non-re-occurring closing costs. The money you get reduces the cash requirement for closing. Remember that closing costs are not deductible (only points paid on a purchase are,) and they cannot be included above the LTV you reach unless it is an FHA loan. Most of the time, you can't have an 80% loan plus closing costs without paying PMI on your loan.

REFINANCES

It Costs to Wait

Nothing is free. Water, once free, costs more in the stores than a can of coke. Air, at a gas station, commonly costs a quarter. Procrastination, no exception to this rule, can cost you a bundle.

If you can refinance, do it. The opportunity to shorten your amortization or just plain save money is one you can't pass up. The loss is equal to the monthly savings you gave up times the length of time you don't act.

If you are attempting to shorten your amortization and don't act, you cannot make up the time once it is gone without making additional payments, which is an additional cost or outlay any way you slice it.

What if you want a rate and the rate available doesn't get you to your target? I have seen many people wait past financially "responsible times" and then chase the rate up until the savings aspect is completely gone. Be wise, be prudent and don't fail to act.

Maximize Your Mortgage Payments

Never, I repeat, never, use your house to save money by reducing your payments unless you really need to have money to survive. Did I say "never?" Never. Ever.

Always, I repeat again, always keep your payment the same when you refinance to a lower interest rate or shorter amortization (assuming the new payment would be lower than the old payment).

It's tempting to take the monthly savings so you can wear it like bragging rights, but your smart friends will interrupt the words "I refinanced to a lower monthly payment" as "I'm kind of dumb and I hope you are, too."

Play it smart, and you'll be able to pay off your mortgage years sooner without any additional effort on your part.

Then you can talk about savings. You won't have any payment on your mortgage. That's what I call bragging rights. Maximize your real savings by ridding yourself of your mortgage. This not only allows you to save, invest or spend additional monies; it secures an asset of yours for future years. Many people have supplemented retirement funds with the monies from the sale of their home. Just think how refreshing it would be to sell your home without having a loan to pay off with part of the proceeds.

Two Steps to a Goal is O.K.

The goal of home ownership without a mortgage is or should be #1 on every homebuyer's list. If it takes a couple refinances to accomplish this, so be it! You might notice people at times bragging about a new lower interest rate, but the quiet person not saying a word is the one without a mortgage who should be the only one bragging. Just in case you don't realize it, a mortgage is a debt you own, and nothing to be bragging about. Should you be on a 30-year fixed and realize, finally, you belong in a 15 year loan but you can't afford the increased payment, consider taking a lower interest short term arm, fixed for three or five years, and maximize your payments (see above).

After 3 or 5 years of maximizing your payment, your balance should be low enough to be able to switch to a 15-year loan without increasing your payment. If it isn't, you could do the exercise again or opt for a slightly higher payment on the 15-year loan.

The net result could be 3 to 5 years' savings or even more. We are talking about 36 to 60 months of not paying your mortgage because there isn't one—it's paid! Set your course to debt-free home ownership without a mortgage—you'll love the results. Now you can do something truly stupid with your money, like invest in some idiotic pyramid scheme and go to jail for a year. You come out, get your comb and wallet, and STILL HAVE A HOUSE!

Be Aware of Loan Limits

Most people know the limit of conforming loans—($417,000 as of present time). Some people have agency jumbos available to ($625,000/max). Jumbos begin at $417,000 when agency jumbos don't exist and $625,000 where they do exist. Jumbo products are more popular in the form of a variable loan, and most likely have a fixed portion as a 3, 5, 7, or 10 year fixed. Fixed loans are available through most jumbo lenders. FHA jumbos go to $729,000/max.

Find out before you act! It could save you a fortune. I'm guessing you like fortunes.

We have lenders that offer conforming rates up to jumbo limits on their portfolio products, while other lenders have jumbo loans up to super jumbo limits generally over one million. Super jumbo limits are up to individual banks.

These portfolio loans are among the best mortgages for most people today. The bigger the loan the more you need to research these limits because an eighth or quarter higher in rates can have a dramatic impact. It's dollars that can be saved, and they're your dollars. And they're not your kids' dollars (no matter how much they think they are). And they're not your ex-spouse's (maybe) or the government's (yet). So hang on to them where you can.

Refinancing Rentals (1-4 units) Doesn't Require Paying Pts.

A lot of people know that there are points associated with rentals also known as "non owner occupied properties." People are aware of this because the lenders want you to know. However, that isn't exactly the whole truth. The fact is, there's a cost to non-owner occupied loans that doesn't exist on owner occupied loans. The cost is usually 1.75% in fee, up to 75% loan to value, and 3 percent over 75% which means about ¼-½% higher in the interest rate. 2-4 units require an additional 1% in fee. Most, if not all, of the costs of a non-owner occupied loans can be covered by raising the interest rates 1/8-1/4%. We do have lenders who will waive the fees up to a $650,000 loan if you take an ARM.

Bottom line in this section: Don't accept a cost. It's not good dollars and cents.

Don't trade a 30 year loan for a 30 year loan

Unless, of course, you're under 10 years of age. If you are under ten years of age, I commend you for reading such a heady book. Now go outside and play.

If you're older and use this course of action, you will never pay off your loan which could be a strategy if planned. If it's not planned, it will become an unplanned reality.

Although mortgage loans are "simple interest" loans, with interest being paid only on the outstanding balance, there is minimal amortization on a 30 year in the first 10 years. (5% in the first 5 years and about a total of 12% in the first 10 years).

When you refinance to save money, you are losing money every month because of the additional payments you need to make as you start the loan over. Plus, you have all 360 months to go.

For example, you have paid for 5 years on a $300,000 @ 4.875%, your payments are $1,610. To complete the 30 years, you have to pay a total of $483,000.

Should you refinance to 30 years @ 3.75% with payments of $1,277, you would pay $459,000 to complete the 30 years. You think you won? Nope, you lose! Even though it appears that you would have substantial monthly savings and some total overall savings, you forgot that after that 25 years you worked hard having to make payments to the bank, they actually could gone to you. Sure, you can now buy brand-name cheese instead of the crap you've been picking up, but that cheese, on the back end, will cost you tens of thousands of dollars. It'd better be damn good cheese.

The only way to survive this mistake is to maximize your mortgage (see above) or take a 20 year loan. 20 years @ 3.625% = $1612/month for a total of $386,880.

Nothing Beats a Low Interest Rate

I have been privy to all kinds of schemes to pay off your mortgage, but guess what? Nothing beats a refinance to a lower interest rate. That's it.

When trying to achieve maximum amortization with an interest rate that is too high, you end up short changing yourself. Extra payments, bi-monthly payments, paying the next month's principal, all pale to paying your mortgage regularly with a lower interest rate.

What can help, though, is taking some of these and putting them into action after you lower your rate. Now you have a cost effective, aggressive attach on your loan balance.

Do not take this lightly. While there are costs to refinance, they are minor especially when compared to trying to make your plan work with a higher interest rate. What was that about a silk purse and a sow . . . ?

<u>Tax Deductibility-When?</u>

Too often, we refinance, pull cash out, and assume that the interest is deductible. Most of the time, you'll be O.K. but not always.

Congress is continually changing the tax laws and home residences are not exempt. Remember that there are a lot of lawyers in office with a lot of time on their hands.

There is a maximum loan amount that is deductible regardless if it's a purchase money mortgage, a refinance, or cash out transaction. Check with your accountant or financial advisor,.

There is also a maximum deductible amount in cash out transactions. Regardless of what you paid for the property, you can only have a set amount above your current mortgage and have it be deductible. But I suggest to you again to check with your accountant or financial advisor.

Private Mortgage Insurance (PMI) is not tax deductible while second deeds or home equity lines of credit are deductible, unless it violates the aforementioned rules.

Don't assume. An audit could find you in a lot of trouble. Imagine having to re-finance to pay the IRS fines. And you really don't want to pay your mortgage with after tax dollars. It isn't pretty. And while we're talking about paying your mortgage with after tax dollars, check out the chart below and see why the least is the best and the most is the worst. It's kind of like looking at a stock chart upside down.

Streamlining Wherever Possible

Many FHA and VA lenders have developed programs that are known as streamlining. These are refinances of existing loans at market or below market rates with minimal costs. They only refinance the current balance, without allowing you to increase your balance by taking cash out. In many cases, the title cannot have been changed in any way over a 24-month period for the lender to allow this type of refinance.

Generally, income documentation is not needed as long as payment on the mortgage has been made on time and credit history is okay. The credit history need not be spectacular.

There are great loans available out there that save both time and money. Be careful of prepayment penalties and unusual terms on these loans. Words like "for the rest of your life," for instance, and "or your first born" should raise a red flag.

__Change Your Life (Style)__

We all want everything now! It's human nature. We stand in front of the microwave and yell "hurry up"! Why not shake up the gods and do something that's contrary to human nature and aim for nothing now and something tomorrow? Sure, now won't be as great as you had hoped but when tomorrow comes it will be phenomenal and now will be just be another yesterday. Read that sentence a couple more times, it'll make sense.

Everyone should try to pay off his or her house loan in one decade. It probably will mean no new cars during that time, few fancy restaurants and inexpensive vacations, clothes and everything else that costs expendable dollars. It means you grind your own coffee beans. It means you mow your own lawn. It's a little bit of pain, relatively speaking.

Tomorrow, a short decade away, your life will change. No more payments and money to spend everywhere. Your friends' new cars from ten years a ago will be old. You'll upgrade your computer every year, for no particular reason. You'll get a satellite dish and sign up for a hundred thousand channels. You'll start going to that cool grocery store down the street where the fruit is stacked neatly and is, for some secret reason, actually fresh. And none of this will equal the amount of your old mortgage payment. If a decade doesn't work, how about 1.5 or 2 decades? Not quite as good, but better than 3 decades. It's your life; I would like to see you enjoy it!

AN EYE OPENER!

$350,000 Loan

Balance	3.000% **15 Yr.**	3.500% **20Yr.**	3.75% **30Yr.**
	$2,417/mo	$2,029/mo	$1,620/mo
5 Yr.	$250,000	$283,900	$315,300
10 Yr.	$134,500	$205,272	$273, 400
15 Yr.	$ 0	$111,581	$222,900

Rules of Thumb(s)

In the mortgage business, the "rule of thumb" and the "old wives tales" are not applicable. When people tell me that no one should refinance unless they lower their payment by 2 percentage points, I laugh—sometimes out loud. Point in case, on a $30,000 loan, it probably wouldn't help and on an $800,000 loan, ½ point would suffice.

You DNA and your mortgage needs are both personal. Thank your advisors for their rules, and then ignore them. If they question you, hand them a book.

Truth-In-Lending Statements

Two forms required by law to be sent out to the
borrower are Truth-In-Lending Statements and Good
Faith Estimates of Costs. These forms are fraught
with problems. First the Truth-In-Lending: this form
is designated to outline the program you and your
loan officer discussed. Generally, either the lender
enters the wrong program (explanation to follow) or
you've changed programs since you filled out your
application. You'll be as frustrated as a cow on an
ice rink.

Next the dreaded Good Faith Estimate of Costs.
Somehow, everyone misses the word estimate.
What they see is not what they were told and, even
worse, it says sign and return. (Not needed). Your
actual costs will be on the closing statement when
you sign your docs before funding your loan. Dodd
Frank, purveyors without credentials, have taken this
problem with their financial regulations and made
sure that everyone who gets a good faith estimate
will become an instant adviser of their loan officer.

Every debt and credit will be on the document and everyone isn't an accountant.

They also took the disclosures which were 3 to 5 pages that nobody read and turned them into the size of an airplane magazine.

What generally throws people the most, though, are taxes, insurance, and prepaid interest. These again are estimates, and if you already have insurance, then you should disregard the lender's estimates. Taxes are for the period you will have the property until the new tax bill is sent while prepaid interest is for the balance of time between the closing and the end of the month. Lenders want all payments to be due on the first of the month and interest is paid in arrears. So if you close on the 15th of the month, you have 15 days of prepaid interest to get to the end of the month and then your first payment would be at the first of the following month. Personally speaking, no matter what I tell my clients in advance, they will always call me when this packet of papers arrives in the mail.

Note from above: Many lenders farm out the Truth-In-Lending and Good Faith Estimate to an outside company. That's why few are ever correct. The law is that they must be sent. No one mentions whether they should be right. Wouldn't it be nice if we could have that same law for, say, taxes?

If points appear and you aren't supposed to pay any, then call your loan officer and see what's up. Try, and I do mean try, not to be upset when the packet arrives. It will save you and your loan officer aggravation and might even lower your blood pressure.

Consider All your Interest Accounts—Not Just Your Mortgage

In today's complex society, many people have different types of interest accounts—from home mortgages to auto, personal, and boat loans as well as a parcel full of credit cards. The average person segregates these accounts into home mortgage and everything else.

The cheapest money is mortgage money and, therefore, if possible, all accounts should be folded into the home mortgage because obviously the interest is lower. There are other reasons. Home loans are deductible except in certain instances and most of the others are not.

People worry that combining will mean that they will be paying their loans and credit cards over a longer period as long as 30 years. It doesn't have to be that way. If you keep your payment the same (including what you have been paying on the credit cards) you will pay those loans and credit cards off even faster because of the lower interest rate.

The very best thing to do is to find your balance on all your obligations and your monthly payments. Then find the shortest amortizing fixed rate loan that has a monthly payment that corresponds to your total monthly payment. That should be your loan of choice. You will realize that all your "other" debt with higher interest rates when rolled together with

your mortgage allows you to pay off your residence
years earlier without changing your life style at all.
Now you ask what was Houdini doing escaping
from bondage instead of mortgage debt?

A home mortgage is your friend.

GENERAL

This means non-specific and applicable to everyone. It doesn't mean unimportant. Don't skip this section because, quite frankly, these are the really great ideas in the book. I know what you're thinking . . . . "They get better?"

Stated Income, Stated Assets . . . O.K.

Over the years, the lenders have devised new and improved methods to assess your riches without massive documentation (think of the trees we're saving). The result have been easier qualifying criteria and more people being able to process mortgage financing.

One of the newest and easily the most popular way to do this is by allowing the borrower to simply state what they earn and what they have in liquid reserves, cash or assets readily converted to cash (stocks, bonds, gold). This seems too good to be true and now it is. These loans as we knew them left us in 2009-10 with the financial crisis.

However, they're back and even easier than before, but only for those who are 62 years of age or older. The only qualification is your age and the fact that you are an owner of a personal residence of 1-4 units. The amount of the loan is determined by your age and the value of your residence.

See "the rest of the story" in the section titled specialty loans.

Now we can only pray for the return of the good old days (didn't say bad old days or mediocre old days,) and the re-opening of the stated loan.

Points, Yeah or Nay?

Points are okay on a purchase (see purchase) and usually don't make sense on anything else. First, they aren't deductible except on a purchase. Remember, we like deductible. Points are amortized over the life of the loan on a refinance which is beneficial in only one case (see below).

Second, they usually do not make sense from a mathematical stand point. If you take the savings from paying the points and divided that amount into the costs of the points, you will generally find up to a 5-year breakeven. Too long! Sure, five years is short for a life, but it's a long, long time if you're holding your breath. And this is like holding your breath.

One major problem arises when rates drop and you should refinance. If you've paid points and haven't recaptured them, you generally are hesitant to spend additional monies to refinance again even though it makes imminent sense. Then you start to curse. Not good. If you need a write off and this type of write-off exists in the future as it does now, when you refinance you can expense the amortized points as the loan is over.

Don't Run From Prepays

Prepayments penalties are there to give the lender assurance that you won't "get rid" of the loan before they can get their profit. In turn you should get a better than market rate for the inconvenience. The winner in this contest is usually determined by the interest rate climate during the prepayment period. There are a number of states that do not allow prepayment penalties. Currently, prepayment penalties either don't exist or exist for a short period, 6 months or a year.

Closing Costs-Do the Math!

Closing costs, those pesky charges that seem ridiculous, are a fact of life in the mortgage industry that one must live with—period! It's what a traffic ticket is to a red sports car.

Your choice is to pay them or take a no cost loan. The obvious choice is to take a no cost loan. In reality, of course, there is a cost: higher interest rate.

Under the Dodd-Frank law a mortgage originator has to make the same percentage on every size loan, using 1-1.5 points, paid by the lender or the borrower who wants a much lower rate. As rates go up so does the points paid by the lender. Therefore, in most cases, if you take an 1/8 higher there will be enough in the rebate to pay the origination and your closing costs. The originator cannot make more, or less, then was posted with the lender. To understand this, imagine "let's make a deal" played by the 3 blind mice.

In your effort to be frugal, don't be unrealistic. Some conforming loans ($417,000 maximum) are too small to do as no cost loans without increasing the rate an untenable amount on getting a deal. Sometimes the "big guys" do get a break, but the so called "little guys" have much more equity. A loan is a debt not a prize!

A.P.R-Another Problem for Roger

Annual percentage rates—a valiant try at regulating, albeit unsuccessful, by our government. Designed for auto loans and seemingly successful, the A.P.R. was soon mandated for home loans. Unfortunately, it doesn't work for a number of reasons:

1. All lenders use different criteria.

2. Different loans are impossible to compare (for ex. variable vs. fixed.)

3. Length of time you keep the loan realistically changes the A.P.R.

Basically, the lender can't be certain about the various adjustments in interest rate so they generally only make one adjustment and use that for their A.P.R.

Don't you just love when the government meddles?

All truth in lending statements have A.P.R.'s which means every client sees this meaningless attempt to satisfy government regulations and calls in disbelief to claim this isn't the interest rate that was quoted to him or her. They're right, of course. Send another check to your local congressman and thank him/her for this silly problem.

<u>Too Good to Be True-Generally Is</u>

My question is why advertise something that isn't true only to have an irate client when they find the truth about the loan. Lenders often count on stupidity. That's why they call you 18 times a day hoping you'll forget you said no 17 times already.

I have listed five of the most common hood-winkers so you might be alert for these or variations thereof.

NUMBER 1

Deception is the ad that reads "30 year amortization" making you believe that its fixed for that period at a rate at least ½% under the market. When you call you find it only fixed for 1 to 3 years which is not exactly what you had in mind.

NUMBER 2

Look out for a low fixed rate and a high A.P.R. Although I am not crazy about A.P.R.'s, in this case, it shows a loan that will have 2 or 3 points. If more is such a good deal then why not advertise the low rate and the high points?

NUMBER 3

"We don't charge points" but somehow we do have a fee that is equal to a point or some fraction of a point. A point is a point no matter what you call it. They might as well call it "screw the buyer charge."

NUMBER 4

In a rising market, advertising rates from days earlier with the effective date in the smallest print. What can I say?

NUMBER 5

Advertising rates you can't lock! It reminds me of the meat market that had low price on ground round, except they were out of it. I'm sure you know that story. It's the classic bait and switch. You came for the Victoria Secret model and they give you one of those freaky "I've got a disease" models that are in the trendy magazines.

More and more lenders are advertising rates that are barley on the rate sheet and certainly not without cost, although they advertise they are without costs. When you get your paperwork, which includes disclosures, you will see a statement that says: "We will not lock the loan until your loan is approved and ready for docs." At that time you will get the rate that is available and most likely not what they advertised.

Go with someone you can trust when it comes time to get a mortgage.

Variable or Fixed-What's for Me?

Should you take a variable rate loan, a fixed rate loan or a hybrid? Not even your mother knows you that well. If someone tells you which you should have before you tell him or her your needs and desires—tell them they need to break up with their boyfriend/girlfriend, sell their car and eat only fish. Act sincere.

To determine what you need, want or desire you must try to answer questions such as the following: How long will you be there? What are your earning prospects? How are your liquid reserves? What's your primary emphasis—low payments or faster amortization? All these are essential to determine which loan is best for you (fixed or variable).

Once you have a clear picture as to the direction you wish to head, you need to analyze your personality. Can you live and or sleep with a variable loan or a short-term fixed that becomes a variable? It's your comfort level that really will determine what your decision should be.

Who said doing the right thing would be easy?

Thirty Years is a Sentence-Not a Loan!

Whoever invented the 30-year loan did the lenders a tremendous service and set consumers back to medieval times. Where is it written that one should pay for their house all their productive days? How'd they pull this scam off?

To begin with, this message is for people 30 years of age to 60 years of age. You can follow even if you do not fall in that age bracket. If you do fall in between the aforementioned numbers, you owe it to yourself not to be caught up in this (sentence) loan. I am not suggesting that if you're younger than 30 or older than 60 that this doesn't apply to you. If you are younger than 30, your only interest is how to get along with the opposite sex, and if you're older than 60, nothing that takes 30 years would interest you.

Fact: A 30 year loan at 3.625% for $300,000 has a fixed payment of $1368.

The 1st payment is made up of $906 interest (66%) and $462 principal (34%).

1. It will take 10.5 years before the above equation will have $684 principal and $684

interest. Compare that with a 20 year loan which has 50.4% interest and 49.6% principal as the makeup of the first payment. It will only take 4 months to be equal. The 15 and 10 year fixed loans are even better than that.

2. If you do not get any benefit from the interest on the 30 year, you are wasting about $80,000 in interest which is 26.6% of the loan. Check with your tax adviser and see how well you would do with the standard deduction instead of itemizing using your home loan interest and real estate taxes. You might be surprised at the outcome.

3. If you purchased the house with 10% down, you will have mortgage insurance for at least 5 years before you reach 80% loan to value. This will cause you more expense that doesn't benefit you financially.

4. If Congress takes away the home mortgage deduction, you will pay an amazing amount of

non-taxable interest which would be similar to rent on your own house because it has no financial value. The total interest on this loan is $192,000 over the 30 years.

5. If you were to take a 15 year loan, the total interest will be $69,700 and will free your payment after 15 years. You then could make the payment to yourself and save $369,700 plus interest. You would be worth twice as much as someone who stays with the 30 year from start to finish.

6. You will pay off a 10 year fixed, a 15 year fixed and 90% of a 20 year fixed before you pay off 1/2 of the 30 year fixed. Need I go on?

7. If you are looking to build your net worth, the 30 year loan will take 11 years to pay off 25% of the loan. This will leave the building of net worth primarily on appreciation and keep you vulnerable to a real estate down turn.

8. The 30 year fixed is the highest interest rate of all the fixed loans—always! It is currently 3/4% higher than a 15 year fixed. This is one time getting high is not good.

9. Doubling up on payments will help pay it off faster. The amount of interest you will pay will still be more than any other fixed loan.

10. You will not be a "rock star" at a cocktail party because so many people either haven't a mortgage or have shorter term mortgages at lower rates. If you are a rock star and have one of these loans, you must be a singer.

Everyone has an Uncle Bob in the family who will be arguing for the 30 year even against all information. If he didn't agree, he wouldn't be Uncle Bob. Unless you hold substantial stock in the banking industry, forget it.

<u>Assumable Loan</u>

There are a number of loans that offer a new
borrower an opportunity to assume the current
loan. This can help you to capture loans that
were taken out at a lower rate than is currently
available, and you can have the lower rate. You
must, however, qualify for the loan even though it
is assumable.

1. ARMS/Variable Loans
   These are loans that are either a straight
   adjustable or have reached the adjustable time
   for these types of loans.

2. FHA Loans
   These are loans available to all Americans
   which allow them to be assumed whether
   fixed or Arms. The downside of these loans
   are that any loan that is amortized over 30
   years has mortgage insurance for the life of
   the loan. If amortized over 15 years, the loan
   has mortgage insurance for 11 years.

The plus to these loans is when interest rates move up they will still be cheaper, even with mortgage insurance, than new loans.

3. VA Loans

   These loans are the best loans we have to offer in America. They are available to active duty military and veterans, and generally offer the lowest rates around without any mortgage insurance. Purchases can be done to 100% of conforming limits without any mortgage insurance. These loans are assumable to anyone, not just active duty military or veterans.

Advertising is 99% on 1 loan—30n Year Conforming Fixed

No one lender has the best rates for every type of loan because no one lender has every type of loan. Yet almost everyone advertises a 30-year fixed for conforming (up to $417,000) owner occupied primary residence.

It's like seeing page after page of people advertising the same Toyota Celica. Odd.

There are over 15 types of 30 year fixed loans and over 250 types of home loans before one really starts to break them down into smaller categories.

How can you judge a lender from their advertisement on one of 15 types on one particular loan? Well, there is one way. The more deceptive they are (see Too Good to Be True) the easier it is to disqualify them from your list of prospective lenders.

I always say if someone is going to cut corners on obvious situations, what are they going to do when it's not so obvious? Saving an eighth in rate can cost you hundreds if not thousands of dollars in costs, lost opportunities or simply being in the wrong loan.

If you are uncomfortable and feel you can't choose the right lender, seek help from your accountant, but not your Uncle Bob! Pretend you have the stomach flu and walk the other way.

The Cocktail Party Problem

I believe most of the serious problems facing this country have come from cocktail parties. Really. No serious subject should ever be allowed to be spoken about during one said party unless the people in the discussion haven't had, nor will they have, anything alcoholic to drink or funny to smoke.

The major problem relating to mortgages is that people misspeak, or forget the facts, or leave out pertinent information or simply deceive their listener about their current or old mortgages. They enforce this by ridiculing, in a clever way, the listener's current or old mortgage. It's like when a drug dealer tells you that drugs really aren't bad for you because he heard it from the guy who sold him his drugs. It's a plethora of bad information.

Almost every irate call I have ever received has come from this situation. Generally, it's from a borrower who has closed a loan and found his friend or an acquaintance at the party who has recently bought or refinanced at a better rate. The answer usually is the friend or acquaintance paid points, got a shorter fixed period load or are within conforming limits (usually 1/4 to 1/2 percent lower) while my borrower didn't pay points and has a larger fixed period jumbo loan.

The anger of my borrower is directly proportionate to the time between discovery and the time we speak.

Caution, please. People are peculiar when it comes to mortgages and very competitive. Don't discuss yours with them and expect to have them quickly admire your superior ability to procure a better loan. This, of course, would mean they would have to admit you are smarter or a better negotiator. Won't happen. You might as well take off your shirt and flex your muscles.

Remember the person standing near you, but not talking, is the one with a house and no mortgage.

That means he or she are the real big wheels at the party, and they already know that.

Big Banks Have Great Rates-For Me?

Banks cannot be beat for rates if you should be the largest depositor in the bank or fill a certain niche—otherwise, not a chance.

Banks can do what they want with customers whenever they want. If you are really important to them, they will be incredibly generous to you in the form of lower rates and cost. If you have 8.5 million in your account and recently saved the life of the banker's child, you should do well. Otherwise, it just doesn't happen often.

Some banks have niches that can work for you. A bank I know loved top ranked entertainers and would beat any deal I could deliver. But if you are a top entertainer or the biggest depositor, do you really need their help? No, but you'll take it, I'm sure.

Other than that, forget about it. I've known business managers who control large amounts of money that are turned down for loans or discouraged from applying for minor flaws. If they can't get favors, how can you?

Don't push our contacts to force them to show you how little you mean to the IR Financial Institution. Take the lunches, free use of a desk and phone, pens, and occasional sleeve of golf balls and be happy.

Did someone once say, "the rich get richer?"

Brokers Cost More Because They Are the "Middlemen"

The aforementioned statement is without a doubt the dumbest thought in the mortgage industry. With the advent of the Internet and the posting of rates on websites, it is even dumber than before everyone saw the current rates!

There are three major variables to line up to make a perfect loan: the borrower, the property, and the loan type.

Now that people are privy to the rates, they are ready to act and cut out the costly middleman.

In a perfect world where all borrowers are the same, all properties are equal, and all loans are equivalent to each other, that would work. Short of that, it doesn't

A borrower is a composite of a credit score, liquid assets and monthly earnings. A property is a composite of its size, type, land, condition and neighborhood. A loan needs to incorporate and be compatible with the conditions.

Rates alone do not serve a borrower in every case because of the aforementioned variable and knowing some of them does not insure the best loan at the lowest interest and least cost for the borrower.

Freely translated, most people who try on their own do not do as well as those who use a broker. It's like reading about a great restaurant dish on the Internet, then going home and trying to cook it. Sure, it may taste okay, but you've missed out on the real flavor if you don't have the right cook.

Don't Accept a Classification of Your Property

Faster than a speeding bullet, lenders will try to take your other property and make it a rental no matter what. The reason is simple—they can charge higher interest and costs.

Do not let this happen. Fight it with all your might. When they try to convince you, close your eyes, put your fingers in your ears, and hum.

There usually is a way around this. Your other property would always be your second home, even if you have 3 or 4 other second homes. Where there is a will, there is a way.

Using a broker (see above) is a start. Most can develop a scenario that will get you that second home designation and save you costs and higher interest.

On conforming or conforming jumbos, there are no up-charges for second homes.

Many lenders today don't up charge for larger second homes and those who do only raise the rates or cost 50% of what rentals are charged. Work with those who are ready, willing and able to work with you.

Keep Your Eye on the Margin

Variable loans are all about indexes and margins. Whatever index is currently popular, you can bet it will be out of favor in a few years and another will take its place.

But I move too fast. A variable loan has a start rate which is predetermined and then is dependent on an index (T-Bill Average, Libor, Cost of Funds, Prime etc.) plus a margin (short for profit margin to the lender) to determine the actual rate.

The index isn't as important as the margin because it's completely out of your control.

The margin really determines your interest rate and is more important than either the start rate or the index.

With all the glare and glitter, rules and regulations of the various variables, (non-negative and potentially negative) one can miss the most important point: the margin.

A low margin is a blessing and can help keep you in this loan for a long time. A high one will eventually force you to refinance.

Nothing beats a lower interest rate (see broker section) and there is no way to get to one without a low margin. Keep those big brown eyes (with cheaters if needed) on the margin.

There is a Loan for Everyone

One thing Wall Street has done for my industry is provide dollars for mortgages of all types. This means lenders have been able to devise loans for the great, near great, so-so, poor, the awful, and the "this-guy-will-be-in-prison-soon" borrowers.

As sure as there are rude people in New York, there is a loan for everyone.

First of all, most people haven't any idea what good or bad credit is for mortgages (see previous section) nor do they have an idea how much money they need to put down on a house should they wish to purchase one.

There isn't a set formula, but I can state there is a loan for everyone. Whether you can live with the terms and conditions is another story.

Owning a home is a start for solving a lot of your financial problems and I always recommend taking the plunge. Once you're in the cycle, generally good things happen that move you toward your ultimate financial goal-independence.

Come on, get aboard and set your sights. Don't worry about the entrance fee. In the long run, it's not only cheap, it's miniscule. You won't even remember it.

Why We Need Sub Prime Loans to Return

Sub Prime loans are not a problem for the financial community—they are a solution.

If you spent an hour on my end of the phone, you would realize the need for these types of loans. The number one question is "why can't I get a loan if I have never missed a payment on my current loan and the new loan will have a lower interest rate and lower payments?" That is certainly not an easy question to give an intelligent answer.

Most people are sure that the entire financial crisis in this country was caused by sub prime loans that created "liar loans" which were stated income loans for wage earners. I never agreed with this nor with the practice when it was used for prime loans as well.

Sub prime loans were less than 10% of all mortgage loans, and the liar loans were probably around 1 to 2% of all mortgage loans. Neither the sub prime, nor the sub prime liar loans caused the financial crisis of 2008-present. What they did do is allow people without traditional sources of income, or great credit or large reserves a chance to get a property and work their way out of their deficiencies.

What they offered were loans that used the deposits for a year or two to be the earnings of the borrower. This means they used the cash flow of the borrower, averaged over a period of time, to determine what they could afford.

Cash flow makes sense, and it worked in sub prime. Obviously those deposits well over the average had to be sourced and proven they were earnings.

Rates were higher, but ratios were expanded a bit. Credit scores were lower. The most popular loan was a 2 year arm, fixed for 2yrs., and amortized over 30 or 40 years. The 2 year arm gave people a chance to clean up their problems and become prime borrowers again.

Our approach to sub prime was to get the borrower enough money out to refinance their mortgage and pay off their other obligations. We didn't stop there because if we did the majority of borrowers would run up their credit cards again. We also gave them enough cash to build a reserve so they wouldn't return to the credit card cycle. For the most part, we were extremely successful, and the borrowers went back to prime mortgages.

Read It and Reap

The box score is designed to allow you to look at the leaders, in loans, that few borrowers ever take the time to do. The box score will show you how the loans work, how long you work for them and how long it takes for the loans to start working for you. Once you digest the information you can ignore it, file it away for future use or let your impulsive side figure a way to put this information to use for you.

The 4 loans that will be featured in the box score are the 30 year fixed, 25 year fixed, 20 year fixed and the 15 year fixed. I have used the current rates for our best borrowers for each loan. The box score will show the payment, the breakdown between principal and interest of the very first payment, the breakdown after 5 years, how long it takes for the principal payment to equal the interest payment and how long to pay off half the loan.

Box Score

Loan	Interest Rate	Mo. Payment	Principal	Interest	Time Factor
30 Year	4.375%	$1498	$404	$1094	1st payment
			$503	$995	61st payment
			$750	$748	14 years, 3 months
25 Year	4.375%	$1640	$552	$1094	1st payment
			$687	$953	61st payment
			$824	$822	9 years, 3 months
20 Year	4.250%	$1858	$795	$1063	1st payment
			$929	$929	3 years, 9 months
15 Year	*3.375%*	*$2126*	*$1282*	*$844*	*1st payment*

The Halfway Point

30 Year   This loan takes 14 years, 3 months to have principal & interest equal. It shouldn't be a surprise that it takes 19 years to pay off half the loan.

25 Year   This loan has the same interest rate as the 30 but only takes 9 years, 3 months for the principal to catch the interest. 15.5 years to payoff half.

20 Year   This loan reaches equality between the principal and interest payments in 3 years, 9 months and pays off half the loan in 12 years.

15 year   This loan has an excess of the payment going to principal from the first payment and pays off half in 8 years, 6 months. That is faster than the 30 year & 25 year needs to reach equality for their principal & interest payment.

Regardless of which loan you choose you only have to pay back $300,000 in principal plus the interest on the loan. The amount of interest is determined by the length of the loan and the interest rate. Although you have seen how long it takes for the principal payment and the interest payment to even up, as well as how long it takes to payoff half of the loan, you still will be surprised at the total interest you pay for the given loan.

	Total Interest	
30 year fixed	$239,226	79.7% of the loan amount
25 year fixed	$193,885	64.6% of the loan amount
20 year fixed	$145,849	48.6% of the loan amount
15 year fixed	$ 82,730	27.5% of the loan amount

Obviously one loan stands out alone as the one most people would choose if they could. There are many reasons to make borrowers shy away from the obvious best loan, but if they concentrate on two facts, they may have the will power to go forward with a shorter loan. Those two facts are as follows: a) the shorter the loan, the lower the overall cost, even if the monthly payment is higher, and b) once you are done with the loan, you have years without payments that can be used for investment instead of paying the additional payments on the loan that has only one thing to offer—a lower monthly payment.

Additional Savings

This is the last table and will show you how much you will save by paying your loan off faster than 30 years. You have already saved money because you have paid a lower amount of interest. This is the amount of the payment you won't make times the months you don't have to pay.

25 year loan	$1640	for 5 years	$98,400
20 year loan	$1858	for 10 years	$222,960
15 year loan	$2126	for 15 years	$382,680

Now that you have seen it in black and white, the "Road to Financial Freedom" awaits.

THE HAIR IS ALMOST GONE

When I entered the mortgage business as the natural adjunct to my real estate brokerage, I didn't realize that the opportunity dwarfed the real estate industries upside, and my beloved Pompadour was on the road to extinction.

It didn't show any signs of the latter point for several years or more. However, early in 1994, after a spectacular year, a steady drop of the mortgage rates from double digits in 1991 to about 6% in 1993, Alan Greenspan started raising interest rates immediately after the Martin Luther King day earthquake in January 1994. I began to notice a hair or two scattered on my desk. My Company and my business started to slow down, followed by a real slow down which got everything retracting beginning March 1, 1994. Things didn't really improve again until June of 1995.

Hair and business began to grow again and only minor problems caused some slow downs and hair loss. I was all smiles as I waited for the changing of the century not realizing that the 3/4 full head of hair was just visiting and not for the long term.

Fast forward to the early 2000's, after 9/11, Andrew Cuomo, now the Governor of New York and formally the head of H.U.D. decided that the mortgage brokers bribed all of the appraisers in the country and got them to inflate their appraisals. He, therefore, came up with a plan to create AMC's, appraisal management companies, to be the middle men between the lenders and the mortgage brokers. Lender's would call the AMC and order an appraisal. The AMC would then order it from an appraiser. Seems simple but there was some serious changes such as the fact that the appraiser isn't given any information to the size of the house or property. If it is a purchase the appraiser gets the purchase contract so there is info on the house and the loan. And, finally, the fee paid to the appraiser is generally substantially lower because the AMC gets a part of the appraisal fee.

The net result of this simple change was the mass exodus of experienced appraisers from the industry and the billions of dollars spent by homeowners for appraisals that did not bring in a value high enough to validate the loan. Hair came out in clumps as given files were torpedoed, but I still was able to part my hair.

Writer's note: The lenders could have ordered a desk review of every appraisal that came in prior to the AMC plan, or a field review of the appraisal or even a second appraisal. For the most part they didn't do it and thus Cuomo found the opening and charged forward. I actually believe he was a co-conspiritor with the Fed to force real estate prices lower.

Then came Barney Frank and Chris Dodd, two politicians who never spent a day in the operations of a mortgage company, but nevertheless felt they had a better way to make sure that all loans would be financially strong. They simply wouldn't be. They created thousands of pages about the day to day operation as they felt it should exist, and most of all they set in motion the loss of the rest of the hair (almost).

They created a rule that requires everyone to "account for" every deposit in their accounts over $1000. "Account for" means a paper trail of where the money originated from. One would think that if a person earned $10,000 a month that they wouldn't have to document the $10,000 a month that is shown on the bank statement. Not necessarily! That is small potatoes compared to the following examples:

1. A borrower with a $1,300,000 loan was looking for a refinance on his house. 7 years earlier, he did some remodeling of a bedroom, and the lender wanted to see a certificate of occupancy after the remodel. He never moved out of the house so there wasn't a certificate of occupancy. We called the building department of his area and also the county and both agreed there wasn't a certificate. His loan to value under 75%.

The appraisal validated the worth of the property but the lender, one of the majors, said no occupancy certificate, no loan.

2. A borrower with a loan just under $1,000,000 and a 65% loan to value with earnings and a retirement account of $1,000,000 plus was declined because he didn't have sufficient non-retirement reserves. His credit score was over 740.

3. A borrower with a house worth (appraised value) $4,500,000 and a loan of $900,000 with a credit score over 740 and $800,000 in reserves was questioned about a deposit of $54,000, as well as another bank statement because it was taking too long. It took to long because they kept asking for one ridiculous condition after another.

Prior to Dodd-Frank all three loans would have been approved in a week. Combined, the three have been worked on over a year and one has still not been approved. This is what we have gained by the never ending useless requirements brought to us by two former politiicans who have bad records when it comes to Fannie Mae and other major lenders.

The stated reason for the bad loans in the past were lack of documentation, lack of sufficient cash down on the purchase, and fraud or lying. We still have FHA loans with 3.5% down, about to go to 5% down, V.A. loans with zero down and a number of ways to buy a house with conventional loans with 5 or 10% down. As for lying and fraud, can you spell Government?

Did You Know?

As I begin to navigate through the mortgage market once again, I feel that half of the craziness in this aspect of finance is because a majority of the industry is built on family tradition. For example, if Grandpa Bill had a 30 year loan, it certainly isn't my place to break the chain of our family by taking a 15 year loan. I will have no relative of mine spinning in their grave over such foolishness of changing the way we pay our home mortgage. Besides it really doesn't matter.

Here are a few facts that you should consider before making your decision:

FACT: The 15 year loan has now reached 2.5% with a small origination charge. At that rate it will amortize 1/2 the loan in 8 years and finish the entire loan in 7 more years by simply making the payments.

FACT: If the 20 year loan was at 2.5%, which it isn't, it would take 11 years to payoff 1/2 of the loan and 9 more years to finish.

FACT: If the 30 year was at 2.5%, which it isn't, it would take 17.5 years to pay off half of the loan and 12.5 years to finish it after the 17.5 years.

And it really doesn't matter!

Paying your loan as a bi-weekly loan (every 2 weeks) allows you to pay it down in approximately 24 years. A simply case of addition will show you that bi-weekly is 26 half payments or 13 whole payments. If you took the 13th payment and made it at the beginning of each year, the mortgage balance would go down at that point and every payment after that would yield a little better amount of amortization. Bi-weekly pays the extra payment over the entire year and doesn't do as well.

Taking cash out of your house is not a taxable event. But, it could cause you to lose part of your new mortgage interest deduction as you cannot deduct anything over your current loan plus $100,000 if the money is used to improve the house.

Back to the 30 year versus a 15 year. The 30 year is a point higher than the 15 year, which should make anyone stop and think about this: 1% more on a 30 year fixed has got to be a lot of money. ($185,000 on a 3.5% $300,000 mortgage). How much more could it be than a 15 year? Three times more:

$300,000, 15 year at 2.5% is $60,000 in interest over the life of the loan.

The real tragedy is the borrowers who take the 30 year and save $650 a month often fail to invest it. If they just stuck it the savings in a mattress in 30 years they would have $234,000. I haven't seen this happen or anything even close to it. The savings, as it turns out, is their road map to enlarging their living. There is nothing wrong with that approach if they have other means for reserves and retirement.

When you purchase a property for cash up until recently you could not refinance the property and take the cash out for at least six months. Now you can, but the value of the property cannot be more than the purchase price and you have to prove that the money you bought it with was your own funds, not borrowed monies.

Finally, a 30 year loan is always the longest loan you can take. It also has the highest interest rate, the slowest amortization, the leader of the pack when rates rise (the follower of the pack when they fall,) and, of course, second in line as the lowest monthly payment, behind interest only loans.

It is BY FAR the most popular loan in America, and I can only ask, "Why?"

GLOSSARY

AMORTIZATION

How to achieve wealth by reducing the balance of your home loan. The lower the interest rate, the faster it amortizes in the beginning of the loan.

APR

Annual Percentage Rate. Impossible to calculate and compare as every lender uses something different in their formula.

BANKRUPTCIES

All of the Chapters of the bankruptcy code 7, 11, 13 must be dismissed for a minimum of two years and credit must be reestablished in order to get an "A" loan. Other types of loans are available with less time and no reestablished credit.

CLOSING AGENT

In charge of all the monies and documents needed to close a purchase transaction or a refinance.

CLOSING COST

The costs to procure a home loan including a title policy, closing agent fee, lender fees, appraisal and credit.

CONFORMING LOANS

Conforming to the rules of FNMA. These loans have a maximum dollar amount that generally increases every year. The dollar amount is broken down by units, 1, 2, 3 or 4. Current single family limit is $252,700. Loans are usually 1/4 percent lower than jumbo's.

COSIGNERS

Old way of helping people qualify for a loan. Today lenders look at the weaker of the two or more borrowers so cosigners usually do not help.

CREDIT SCORE

A number devised by an independent company that will appear on your credit report. The formula is secret and is used to help determine your qualifications for a loan.

DEDUCTIBILITY

The ability to deduct the interest on your home loan from your gross earnings to save income taxes. Generally you can deduct the interest however this is subject to a maximum and also some exceptions. Consult your accountant.

DEEDS IN LIEU

Giving the lender the deed to your house to avoid going through a foreclosure proceeding.

DEED OF TRUST

The recorded instrument that secures the loan from the lender to your property. Used in more states than mortgage. The note is not part of this.

DEFLATION

The phenomenon that causes commodity prices to drop. Usually occurs when the economy of a nation is under performing.

ESCROW COMPANIES

See closing agent.

FORECLOSURE

The action of a lender to take back the property for failure to meet the terms of the loan.

GOOD FAITH ESTIMATE OF COSTS

Sent to the borrower by the lender to give you an idea of the costs of the loan.

GRANT DEED

The instrument that is recorded that transfers ownership from one person or entity to another. Popular forms of grant deeds are Quitclaim Deeds.

HYBRIDS

Variables that are fixed for a period of time: 2 years, 3 years, 5 years, 7 years or 10 years. After the fixed period, the loan becomes a variable for the balance of the term.

INFLATION

More money chasing fewer products causing an increase in prices. Inflation is not a friend to fixed income securities and is the sole reason for rising interest rates.

INDEX

The base figure of a variable loan. It is the financial instrument whose interest rate is used as the basis for a variable loan. Ex: 1 year T-bill, 6 mo. Libor, Prime Rate.

IRS

If you don't know, don't ask.

LOCKING A LOAN

Ideally and usually a one time event when the borrower is content with the rate and terms of the prospective loan and agrees to ease from further negotiations.

LTV

Loan to value. This is the limit you may borrow on the various types of home loans.

LOX

Smoked salmon, usually consumed with bagel and cream cheese.

MARGIN

Short for profit margin. The amount added to the index to determine the interest rate on a variable loan.

MONDAYS

The beginning of the week, the home of Monday Night Football and a terrible day to conclude a real estate transaction involving a new loan.

MORTGAGE

An instrument that is recorded which includes the note and secures the loan from the lender to your property.

NON OWNER OCCUPIED

A property that is not owned by the party residing in it. Generally known as a rental.

PIGGYBACKS

A 1st and 2nd T.D. configuration that brings the LTV over 80% but allows the borrower to use the 2nd T.D. and not pay P.M.I.

POTENTIAL NEGATIVE LOAN

A loan designed to allow payments that are less than the interest only payment. If that option is elected than the loan has a rising balance as the difference between the payment and the interest only payment is added monthly to your balance.

PREPAID INTEREST

Interest on a home loan is paid in arrears. When a loan closes, the 1st pament is due in 30 days. The lenders want all payments due on the 1st of each month and therefore require you to pay prepaid interest from the close to the 1st of the following month. This will assure all payments will be due on the 1st of the month.

PREQUALIFICATIONS

The ability to find out what you can be qualified for in a home loan. This would include the dollar amount as well as the LTV.

PRIVATE MORTGAGE INSURANCE

The insurance lenders seek for the amount of the loan above 80% LTV. The borrowers must pay the premium even though the lender is the intended beneficiary. The insurance will be paid if the property is lost and the lender is not paid.

REPOSSESSIONS

Same as foreclosure.

R.S.

My Mother's #2 son, an aspiring author.

TITLE COMPANIES

Insure the title of the property for the owner and or the lender. Title companies sometimes act as closing agents.

UNCLE BOB

The "maven" or know it all in your family who is quick to advise you on your transaction. Generally the knowledge of this person is inversely proportionate to his or her personality.

VARIABLE INTEREST RATE (HYBRIDS)

The loan whose payment and or interest rate varies at set periods: a month, 6 months or one year. The interest rate is determined by adding the index and the margin subject to yearly and lifetime caps.

About the Author

Roger Schlesinger is the MortgageMinuteGuy who has been heard on over 400 stations in the United States for the last decade and a half and seen on Television through out the country for almost as long.

He has been involved in the real estate industry as a real estate broker and a mortgage broker in several states for decades while also spending his time trying to educate the public through his broadcasts and writings.

Roger has a Bachelor of Arts Degree in Economics from U.C.L.A and a Masters Degree in Finance from U.S.C. Roger has had his own Mortgage Brokerage Company for years, and was affiliated with several mortgage banks for years. He is currently spokesman for a number of mortgage companies.

He can be reached by e-mail at Roger @ MortgageMinuteGuy.com